Design: Jill Coote
Recipe Photography: Peter Barry
Recipe styling: Jacqueline Bellefontaine,
Bridgeen Deery and Wendy Devenish
Jacket and Illustration Artwork: Jane Winton,
courtesy of Bernard Thornton Artists, London
Compiled and introduced by Laura Potts
Edited by Josephine Bacon

Published by
CHARTWELL BOOKS, INC.
A Division of **BOOK SALES, INC.**
110 Enterprise Avenue
Secaucus, New Jersey 07094

CLB 3353
© 1993 CLB Publishing,
Godalming, Surrey, England
Printed and bound in Singapore
ISBN 1-55521-981-0

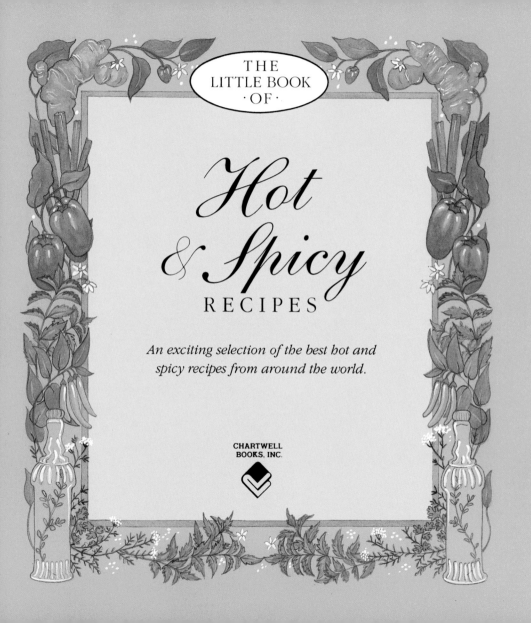

THE LITTLE BOOK ·OF·

Hot & Spicy
RECIPES

An exciting selection of the best hot and spicy recipes from around the world.

CHARTWELL
BOOKS, INC.

Introduction

Spices – the dried seeds, pods, berries, roots, stems, or buds of aromatic plants – play a vital part in the culinary traditions of many nations. In the past, spices were vital both for preserving and flavoring food, and as such were a very valuable commodity. As methods of food preservation have become more sophisticated, however, the value of spices has dropped. This, coupled with the fact that spices are more widely grown and can be more cheaply transported, has seen an increase in the variety of spices that are available and their use in everyday cooking.

A wide selection of pre-ground spices is available in most supermarkets, and are frequently the preferred choice. It is advisable, however, when buying pre-ground spices not to buy too large a quantity, as they lose much of their aroma and flavor if they are stored over a long period of time. This loss of pungency can be avoided, to a degree, by ensuring that the spices are kept out of direct sunlight, either by storing them in tinted glass jars or in a cabinet. Though more time-consuming, grinding spices, as and when you need them, is the best way to get the strongest, truest flavor. Grinding spices can be done either by hand with a pestle and mortar, or in a small coffee grinder, kept specifically for the purpose.

Spices are usually associated with the cuisines of countries where the climate is very hot. This is not simply because this is the climate in which the plants flourish. Spices are still used widely as a preservative, prolonging the time foods can be kept – an important function in hot countries, where vegetables and meats deteriorate rapidly. They also help to stimulate appetites that are flagging in the heat. Fresh or dried chili peppers and cayenne pepper, for example, will add fire to any dish. Yet, food can be spicy without being very hot. Spices such as cumin, coriander, and cinnamon can lend flavor and fragrance to a dish, without being overpoweringly hot.

The recipes in this book come from around the world, and include favorites from Indian, Mexican, and Chinese cuisine. They show the different ways in which herbs and spices are used, and the diversity of delicious flavors that can be achieved with even the simplest mixture of spices.

Hot and Sour Seafood Soup

SERVES 4

This interesting combination of flavors and ingredients makes a sophisticated beginning to an informal meal.

PREPARATION: 20 mins
COOKING: 20 mins

---

3 dried Japanese mushrooms – shiitake
1 tbsp oil
1 cup shrimp, shelled and deveined
1 red chili, seeded and finely sliced
1 green chili, seeded and finely sliced
½ tsp lemon rind, cut into thin slivers
2 green onions (scallions), sliced
2½ cups fish broth
1 tbsp Worcestershire sauce
1 tbsp light soy sauce
1 cup fish fillet, flaked
1 cake tofu, diced
1 tbsp lemon juice
1 tsp sesame seeds
1 tsp fresh coriander (cilantro), finely chopped
(optional)

Step 1 Soak the dried Japanese mushrooms in boiling water about 20 minutes, until they are completely reconstituted.

Step 4 Remove the hard stalks from the Japanese mushrooms and discard them. Slice the caps finely.

1. Soak the mushrooms in enough hot water to cover for 20 minutes, or until completely reconstituted.

2. Heat the vegetable oil in a wok or skillet, and add the shrimp, chilies, lemon rind, and green onions (scallions). Stir-fry quickly 1 minute.

3. Add the stock, the Worcestershire sauce, and the soy sauce. Bring this mixture to the boil, reduce the heat, and simmer 5 minutes. Season to taste.

4. Remove the stalks from the mushrooms and discard them. Slice the caps very finely.

5. Add fish fillet to the soup, together with the bean curd and Japanese mushrooms. Simmer 5 minutes.

6. Stir in the lemon juice and sesame seeds. Adjust the seasoning, and serve sprinkled with chopped fresh coriander leaves, if desired.

Chili Vegetable Soup

SERVES 4

This simple-to-make soup makes a light first course.

PREPARATION: 40 mins
COOKING: 20 mins

Taco Sauce
1 tbsp oil
1 onion, diced
1 green bell pepper, diced
½-1 red or green chili pepper, chopped
½ tsp ground cumin
½ tsp ground coriander (cilantro)
½ clove garlic, crushed
Pinch salt, pepper, and sugar
14 ounces canned tomatoes
Tomato paste

1 tbsp oil
1 onion, chopped
½ cup canned whole green chilies, quartered
2 pints chicken broth
1 large potato, peeled and cut into short strips
1 tbsp lime juice
Tortilla chips and lime slices to garnish

1. Heat the oil in a heavy-based saucepan, add the onion and bell pepper, and cook slowly to soften slightly.

Step 5 Add the remaining ingredients and simmer 20 minutes.

2. Add the chili, cumin, coriander, and garlic and cook a further 2-3 minutes.

3. Add sugar, seasonings, and tomatoes with their juice. Break up the tomatoes with a fork or a potato masher.

4. Cook a further 5-6 minutes over moderate heat to reduce. Add tomato paste for color, if necessary. Season to taste.

5. Heat the remaining oil in a large saucepan and sauté the onion until translucent. Add the chilies, broth, potato, and pre-prepared taco sauce.

6. Cover the pan and simmer soup 20 minutes. Stir in the lime juice and add salt.

7. Serve in individual bowls with tortilla chips. Cut a thin slice of lime to float in each bowl of soup.

Samosas

SERVES 6

These snacks from India can be eaten either hot or cold.

PREPARATION: 40 mins
COOKING: 25 mins

Pastry
2½ cups all-purpose flour
¼ tsp salt
¼ tsp baking powder
Water, to mix

Filling
3 tbsps oil
1 medium onion, chopped
1 pound potatoes, cut into small dice
2 carrots, grated
¼ cup green peas, shelled
¼ cup green beans, chopped
1 tsp chili powder
1 tsp salt
1 tsp garam masala or curry powder
½ tsp ground turmeric
1 tbsp lemon juice
Oil for deep frying

1. Make the pastry by sifting the flour, salt, and baking powder into a bowl and adding enough water, a little at a time, to mix to a soft dough. Cover and leave to stand 30 minutes.

2. Heat the oil and sauté the onion until it is just soft. Stir in the potatoes and carrots and cook 3-4 minutes.

Step 6 Fill each cone with a little of the vegetable mixture.

3. Add the peas and beans to the potato mixture, cook a further 2 minutes, then stir in the spices and lemon juice. Cover and simmer until the potatoes are tender. Remove from the heat and allow to cool.

4. Divide the dough into 12 equal-sized balls. Roll each piece out on a floured board, to a thin circle about 6 inches in diameter.

5. Cut each circle in half. Dampen the straight edges of each semicircle and bring them together, overlapping slightly to make a cone.

6. Fill each cone with a little of the filling, then dampen the open edge and seal by pressing together firmly. For extra firmness dampen and fold this edge over.

7. Heat the oil for frying. Fry the samosas, a few at a time, until they are golden brown. Drain on absorbent kitchen paper.

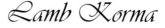

Lamb Korma

SERVES 4

Lamb Korma, a rich, spicy dish, is one of the best known curries from India.

PREPARATION: 15 mins
COOKING: 40-50 mins

3 tbsps oil
1 medium onion, sliced
1-inch piece cinnamon stick
6 cloves
Seeds of 6 small cardamom pods
1 bayleaf
1 tsp black cumin seeds
2 tsps grated ginger root
2 cloves garlic, crushed
1 pound shoulder of lamb, cubed
1 tsp chili powder
1 tsp ground coriander (cilantro)
2 tsps ground cumin
¼ tsp ground turmeric
⅔ cup plain yogurt
¾ cup water
1 tbsp ground almonds
2 green chilies, halved and seeded
2 sprigs fresh coriander (cilantro), chopped

1. Sauté the onion in the oil until golden brown. Add the cinnamon, cloves, cardamom seeds, bayleaf, and the cumin seeds. Sauté 1 minute.

2. Add the ginger and garlic, and the cubed lamb. Sprinkle with the chili powder, ground coriander, cumin, and turmeric and mix together well.

Step 1 Fry the whole spices with the onion 1 minute.

3. Stir in the yogurt, cover the pan, and cook over moderate heat 10-15 minutes, stirring occasionally.

4. Add the water and season, re-cover and simmer gently 30-40 minutes, or until the meat is tender.

5. Just before serving, add the almonds, chilies, and coriander leaves. Stir in a little more water if necessary.

Step 3 Stir the yogurt into the lamb korma, and mix well, to blend thoroughly.

14

Curried Pork Stew

SERVES 4

This savory stew requires long, slow cooking to bring out its flavor.

PREPARATION: 25 mins
COOKING: 1 hr 30 mins

---

2 pounds pork shoulder, cut into 2-inch cubes
2 tbsps oil
2 medium onions, coarsely chopped
1 large green bell pepper, seeded and coarsely chopped
1 tbsp curry powder
2 cloves garlic, crushed
1 pound canned tomatoes
3 tbsps tomato paste
⅔ cup water or beef broth
2 tbsps cider vinegar
1 bayleaf
½ tsp dried mint
A few drops Tabasco sauce

Step 2
Combine the ingredients and stir well to break up the tomatoes slightly.

Step 4 When the meat is tender, skim excess fat from the surface of the sauce with a spoon.

1. Heat about 2 tbsps oil in a large skillet. When hot, add the pork cubes in two batches. Brown over high heat about 5 minutes per batch, then reserve. Add more oil if necessary and cook the onions and peppers to soften. Add the curry powder and garlic and cook 1 minute more.

2. Add the tomatoes, their juice, and the tomato paste. Stir in the water or stock and vinegar breaking up the tomatoes slightly. Add bayleaf, mint, and then season.

3. Transfer to a casserole dish. Bring the mixture to the boil and then cook slowly about 1½ hours, covered.

4. When the meat is tender, skim any fat from the surface of the sauce, remove the bayleaf and add a few drops of Tabasco sauce to taste.

Spare Ribs in Chili and Cream Sauce

SERVES 4

Unsweetened cocoa lends color and depth to a sauce for ribs.

PREPARATION: 20 mins
COOKING: 50-55 mins

2¼ pounds spare ribs
1 tsp cocoa powder
1 tbsp all-purpose flour
½ tsp cumin
½ tsp paprika
½ tsp dried oregano, crushed
1¼ cups warm water
2 tbsps liquid honey
2 tbsps heavy cream
Lime wedges and watercress for garnish

---

1. Leave the ribs in whole slabs and roast at

Step 1 Cook the ribs until well browned. Remove from the roasting pan and drain the fat.

Step 3 Place ribs on a chopping board and cut into pieces.

400°F 20-25 minutes, or until well browned. Drain off all the excess fat.

2. Blend together the cocoa, flour, cumin, paprika, oregano, water, and honey, and season well. Pour mixture over the ribs. Lower the oven temperature to 350°F and cook ribs for a further 30 minutes, until the sauce has reduced and the meat is tender.

3. Cut the ribs into pieces and arrange on a serving platter.

4. Pour the cream into the sauce in the roasting pan and place over moderate heat. Bring to the boil and pour over the ribs.

5. Garnish with lime wedges and serve.

Albóndigas (Meatballs)

SERVES 4

These hot, spicy meatballs make a tasty supper dish.

PREPARATION: 25 mins
COOKING: 20 mins

8 ounces ground veal
8 ounces ground beef
1 clove garlic, crushed
2 tbsps dry breadcrumbs
½ chili pepper, seeded and finely chopped
½ tsp ground cumin
1 egg, beaten
3 tbsps oil
1¼ cups Taco Sauce (see Chili Vegetable Soup)
2 green onions (scallions), chopped

1. Mix together the veal, beef, garlic, breadcrumbs, chili pepper, cumin, and season well. Add the egg gradually until well-blended.

Step 3 Flour hands well and roll each piece into a ball.

Step 5 Brown the meatballs on all sides in hot oil until a good color.

2. Turn the mixture out onto a floured surface and divide into 16 equal pieces.

3. With floured hands, shape the mixture into balls.

4. Pour about 3 tbsps of oil into a large skillet and place over high heat.

5. When the oil is hot, add the meatballs and sauté 5-10 minutes until brown on all sides. Turn frequently during cooking.

6. Remove the browned meatballs and drain well on paper towels. Place in an ovenproof dish and pour over the taco sauce.

7. Heat through in a preheated 350°F oven for 10 minutes. Sprinkle with chopped onions to serve.

Chili Beef Stew

SERVES 6-8

Red onions, red bell peppers, tomatoes, and red beans all go into this zesty stew.

PREPARATION: 25 mins
COOKING: 1-2 hrs

2 pounds chuck steak, cut into 1-inch pieces
4 tbsps oil
1 large red onion, coarsely chopped
2 cloves garlic, crushed
2 red bell peppers, seeded and roughly
   chopped
1-2 red chilies, seeded and finely chopped
3 tbsps mild chili powder
1 tbsp cumin
1 tbsp paprika
3¾ cups beer, water or broth
1 cup canned tomatoes, puréed
2 tbsps tomato paste
1 cup canned red kidney beans, drained
Pinch salt
6 ripe tomatoes, peeled, seeded, and diced

Step 2 If using beer, add it very slowly as it will tend to foam up in the heat of the pan.

Step 2 Cook the onions, garlic, red bell peppers, and chilies slowly until slightly softened.

1. Pour the oil into a flameproof casserole or Dutch oven. When hot, brown the meat in small batches over moderately high heat about 5 minutes per batch.

2. Reserve the meat on a plate. Reduce the heat and cook the onion, garlic, red peppers, and chilies about 5 minutes. Add the chili powder, cumin, and paprika, and cook 1 minute further. Pour on the liquid and add the canned tomatoes, tomato paste, and the meat.

3. Cook slowly about 1½-2 hours. Add the beans about 45 minutes before the end of cooking time.

4. When the meat is tender, add salt to taste and serve garnished with diced tomatoes.

Tamarind Chicken Satay

SERVES 4

Tomato and chili sambal makes the perfect accompaniment for this dish.

PREPARATION: 30 mins
COOKING: 10-15 mins

---

4 chicken breasts, skinned, boned, and cut into
 ½-inch cubes

Marinade
1 tbsp oil
2-inch piece tamarind, soaked in ½ cup hot
 water or lemon juice
2 cloves garlic, crushed
1 tsp ground cardamom
½ tsp grated nutmeg
Salt and pepper
1 tsp sweet soy sauce

Tomato and Chili Sambal
2 red chili peppers
1 small piece fresh ginger, grated
1 clove garlic, crushed
1 pound fresh tomatoes, peeled and seeded
4 tbsps oil
1 tbsp lemon or lime juice
1 tbsp dark brown sugar
Salt and pepper

---

1. Put the chicken in a large bowl. Mix together
the marinade ingredients and pour them over
the chicken. Stir well and refrigerate for at least
30 minutes.

Step 6 Cook the chicken skewers. Baste them with the remaining marinade as they cook.

2. Grind together the chilies, ginger, and garlic.
Chop the tomatoes coarsely and blend them
into the chili mixture.

3. Heat the oil in a wok or large skillet and fry
the tomato mixture about 5-6 minutes, stirring
occasionally to prevent it sticking. Add the
lemon juice and a spoonful of water if the sauce
becomes too thick.

4. Stir in the sugar and season to taste.

5. Thread the marinated chicken cubes onto
thin wooden skewers.

6. Cook the chicken under a preheated broiler,
turning frequently, until golden brown, about
5-8 minutes. Brush the chicken with the
remaining marinade during cooking.

Plaice with Spicy Tomato Sauce

SERVES 4

This piquant fish dish is popular along Mexico's Gulf coast.

PREPARATION: 30 mins
COOKING: 20-25 mins

½ package cream cheese
1 tsp dried oregano
Pinch cayenne pepper
4 whole fillets of plaice
Lime slices and dill to garnish

Tomato Sauce
1 tbsp oil
1 small onion, chopped
1 stick celery, chopped
1 chili pepper, seeded and chopped
¼ tsp each ground cumin, coriander, and ginger
½ red and ½ green bell pepper, seeded and chopped
14 ounces canned tomatoes
1 tbsp tomato paste
Salt, pepper, and a pinch sugar

1. Heat the oil in a heavy-based pan and cook the onion, celery, chili pepper, and spices about 5 minutes over very low heat.

2. Add the remaining ingredients and bring to the boil. Reduce heat and simmer 15-20 minutes, stirring occasionally. Set aside.

Step 6 Spread cheese filling on the fish and roll up each fillet.

3. Mix the cream cheese, oregano, and cayenne pepper together, and set aside.

4. Skin the fillets, starting at the tail end and holding the knife at a slight angle to the skin.

5. Push the knife along using a sawing motion, with the blade against the skin. Dip fingers in salt to make it easier to hold onto the fish skin. Gradually separate the fish from the skin.

6. Spread the cheese filling on all 4 fillets and roll each up. Secure with cocktail sticks.

7. Place the fillets in a lightly-greased baking dish, cover and cook 10 minutes in a preheated 350°F oven.

8. Pour the tomato sauce over the fish and cook a further 10-15 minutes. Fish is cooked when it feels firm and looks opaque. Garnish with lime slices and dill.

Coconut Fried Fish with Chilies

SERVES 4

A real treat for lovers of spicy food.

PREPARATION: 30 mins
COOKING: 30 mins

Oil for frying
1 pound sole or plaice fillets, skinned, boned
    and cut into 1-inch strips
Seasoned flour
1 egg, beaten
½ cup grated or flaked coconut
1 tbsp vegetable oil
1 tsp grated fresh ginger root
¼ tsp chili powder
1 red chili, seeded and finely chopped
1 tsp ground coriander (cilantro)
½ tsp ground nutmeg
1 clove garlic, crushed
2 tbsps tomato paste
2 tbsps tomato chutney
2 tbsps dark soy sauce
2 tbsps lemon juice
2 tbsps water
1 tsp brown sugar
Salt and pepper

1. In a skillet, heat about 2 inches of oil to 375°F. Toss the fish strips in the seasoned flour and then dip them into the beaten egg. Roll them in the coconut and shake off the excess.

Step 1 Toss the strips of fish in the flour and then dip them in the beaten egg. Roll them finally in the dry coconut.

2. Fry the fish, a few pieces at a time, in the hot oil and drain them on absorbent kitchen paper. Keep warm.

3. Heat the 1 tbsp oil in a wok or skillet and sauté the ginger, red chili, spices, and garlic, about 2 minutes.

4. Add the remaining ingredients and simmer about 3 minutes. Serve the fish, with the sauce handed round separately.

Step 2 Sauté the fish in the hot oil, a few pieces at a time, to prevent it from breaking up.

Cod Curry

SERVES 4

The fragrant spices used in this recipe complement the fish perfectly.

PREPARATION: 15 mins
COOKING: 20 mins

3 tbsps vegetable oil
1 large onion, finely chopped
1-inch piece cinnamon stick
1 bayleaf
1 tsp ginger paste
1 tsp garlic paste
1 tsp chili powder
1 tsp ground cumin
1 tsp ground coriander
¼ tsp ground turmeric
⅔ cup plain yogurt OR
1 cup canned tomatoes, chopped
1-2 fresh green chilies, chopped
2 sprigs fresh coriander leaves, chopped
1 tsp salt
1 pound cod cutlets, or fillets, cut into
    2-inch pieces

1. In a large, heavy-based saucepan, sauté the onion in the oil until golden brown. Add the cinnamon, bayleaf, ginger and garlic pastes, and fry 1 minute.

2. Add the ground spices and sauté for a further minute, then stir in *either* the yogurt, *or* the canned tomatoes and the chopped chilies, and coriander leaves.

Step 1 Fry the cinnamon, bayleaf, the ginger paste, and garlic paste with the onions 1 minute.

3. Only if you have used yogurt, stir in ⅔ cup water and simmer the mixture 2-3 minutes. Do not add any water if you have used the canned tomatoes.

4. Stir the cod into the sauce, and add the salt. Cover the pan and simmer 15-18 minutes before serving.

Step 4 Add the cod pieces to the sauce in the pan, stir well to coat thoroughly, before covering and simmering 15-18 minutes.

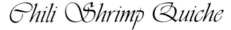

Chili Shrimp Quiche

SERVES 6

Fresh chili peppers give a Mexican flavor to this quiche.

PREPARATION: 40 mins, including time for the
  dough to chill
COOKING: 30-40 mins

Pastry
1 cup all-purpose flour
Pinch salt
2 tbsps butter or margarine
2 tbsps Crisco
2-4 tbsps cold water

Filling
4 eggs
⅔ cup milk
⅔ cup pint single cream
½ clove garlic, crushed
½ cup yellow cheese, grated
3 green onions (scallions), chopped
2 green chilies, seeded and chopped
1 cup cooked and peeled shrimp
Cooked, unpeeled shrimp and parsley sprigs
  for garnish

---

1. Sift the flour with a pinch of salt into a
mixing bowl.

2. Rub in the butter and fat until the mixture
resembles fine breadcrumbs.

3. Mix in the liquid gradually, adding enough
to bring the dough together into a ball.

4. Wrap the dough well and chill 30 minutes.

Step 6 Use the rolling pin to help lift the dough into the flan dish.

5. Roll out the dough on a well-floured surface
with a floured rolling pin.

6. Wrap the dough around the rolling pin to lift
it into a 10-inch flan dish.

7. Carefully press the dough onto the bottom
and up the sides of the dish.

8. Roll the rolling pin over the top of the dish
to remove excess dough.

9. Mix the eggs, milk, cream, and garlic together
and lightly season. Sprinkle the cheese, green
onion, chilies, and shrimp onto the base of the
dough and pour over the egg mixture.

10. Bake in a preheated 400°F oven for 30-40
minutes until firm and golden brown. Peel the
tail shells off the shrimp and remove the legs
and roe if present. Use the shrimp to garnish
the quiche along with the sprigs of parsley.

Egg Curry

SERVES 4

Quick and easy, this curry is a delicious way of serving hard-cooked eggs.

PREPARATION: 10 mins
COOKING: 20 mins

4-6 eggs
1 large onion, finely chopped
1 tbsp oil
1-inch stick cinnamon
1 bayleaf
4 small cardamom pods
6 cloves
1 tsp garlic paste
1 tsp ginger paste
1 tsp ground coriander
1 tsp ground cumin
¼ tsp ground turmeric
1 tsp garam masala or curry powder
1 tsp chili powder
1 cup canned tomatoes, crushed
Salt to taste
¾ cup water or vegetable broth
2 sprigs fresh coriander (cilantro) leaves
2 green chilies

1. Hard-cook the eggs 8-10 minutes. Cool them completely in cold water, then remove the shells.

2. Heat the oil in a large saucepan and sauté the onion gently until it is soft, but not browned.

Step 5 Put the hard-cooked eggs into the curry sauce, stir well and cook 10-12 minutes.

3. Add the cinnamon, bayleaf, cardamoms, and cloves, and fry 1 minute. Stir in the ginger and garlic pastes. Add the coriander, cumin, turmeric, garam masala, and chili powder. Stir together well and fry 30 seconds.

4. Add the tomatoes and salt to the spices. Stir in well and simmer 5 minutes. Add the water or broth, and bring the mixture to the boil.

5. Put the eggs into the curry sauce and simmer 10-12 minutes.

6. Chop the coriander leaves and the green chilies finely, and sprinkle them over the cooked eggs, to garnish.

Penne with Spicy Chili Sauce

SERVES 4-6

Penne are hollow pasta tubes which can be bought at most supermarkets.

PREPARATION: 15 mins
COOKING: 30 mins

1 pound canned tomatoes
1 tbsp olive oil
2 cloves garlic, crushed
1 onion, chopped
4 slices Canadian bacon, chopped
2 red chili peppers, seeded and chopped
2 green onions (scallions), chopped
¼ cup Parmesan cheese, grated
1 pound penne
Salt and pepper

Step 5 Toss the cooked penne in half of the sauce, mixing together well to coat evenly.

Step 3 Stir the sieved tomatoes, chili peppers, green onions, and half the cheese into the onion mixture.

1. Chop the tomatoes and sieve them to remove the seeds.

2. Heat the oil in a skillet and fry the garlic, onion, and bacon gently 6-8 minutes.

3. Add the sieved tomatoes, the chili peppers, green onions, and half of the cheese. Simmer gently 20 minutes.

4. Cook the penne in boiling water 10-15 minutes. Rinse under hot water and drain well.

5. Put the cooked penne into a warm serving platter and toss them in half of the sauce. Pour the remaining sauce over the top and sprinkle with the remaining cheese.

Spicy Rice and Bean Pilaf

SERVES 6-8

This recipe can either be served as a side dish or vegetarian main course.

PREPARATION: 25 mins
COOKING: 50 mins

4 tbsps oil
1 cup long grain rice
1 onion, minced
1 green bell pepper, seeded and chopped
1 tsp each each ground cumin and coriander
  (cilantro)
Dash Tabasco sauce
Salt
1¾ pints vegetable broth
1 pound canned red kidney beans, drained
1 pound canned tomatoes, drained and
  coarsely chopped
Chopped parsley

Step 2 Cook the rice in the oil until just turning opaque.

Step 3 Cook with the remaining ingredients until rice is tender and most of the liquid is absorbed.

1. Heat the oil in a casserole or large saucepan.

2. Add the rice and cook until just turning opaque. Add the onion, pepper, cumin, and coriander. Cook gently a further 2 minutes.

3. Add the Tabasco, salt, broth, beans, and bring to the boil. Cover and cook about 45 minutes, or until the rice is tender and most of the liquid has been absorbed.

4. Remove from the heat and add the tomatoes, stirring them in gently. Leave to stand, covered, for 5 minutes.

5. Fluff up the mixture with a fork and sprinkle with parsley to serve.

Oriental Noodles

SERVES 4

A most versatile vegetable dish, this goes well with meat or can stand alone.

PREPARATION: 25 mins
COOKING: 7-8 mins

---

8 ounces Chinese noodles (medium thickness)
5 tbsps oil
4 carrots, peeled
1 cup broccoli
12 Japanese mushrooms (shiitake), soaked 30 minutes
1 clove garlic, peeled
4 green onions (scallions), diagonally sliced
1-2 tbsps chili sauce, mild or hot
4 tbsps soy sauce
4 tbsps rice wine or dry sherry
2 tsps cornstarch

Step 7 Cook vegetables and sauce ingredients until cornstarch thickens and clears.

1. Cook noodles in boiling, salted water for about 4-5 minutes. Drain well, rinse under hot water, and drain again. Toss with 1 tbsp of the oil to prevent sticking.

2. Slice the carrots thinly on the diagonal.

3. Cut the flowerets off the stems of the broccoli and divide into even-sized but not too small sections. Slice the stalks thinly on the diagonal.

4. Place the vegetables in boiling water about 2 minutes to blanch. Drain and rinse under cold water.

5. Remove and discard the mushroom stems and slice the caps thinly.

6. Heat a wok and add the remaining oil with the garlic clove. Leave the garlic in the pan while the oil heats and then remove it. Add the carrots and broccoli and stir-fry about 1 minute. Add mushrooms and onions and continue to stir-fry, tossing the vegetables in the pan continuously.

7. Combine chili sauce, soy sauce, wine, and cornstarch. Pour over the vegetables and cook until the sauce clears. Toss with the noodles and heat them through and serve immediately.

Eggplant and Peppers Szechuan Style

SERVES 4

Authentic Szechuan food is fiery hot. Outside China, restaurants often tone down the taste for Western palates.

PREPARATION: 30 mins
COOKING: 7-8 mins

---

1 large eggplant
2 cloves garlic, crushed
1-inch piece fresh ginger, finely chopped
1 onion, roughly chopped
1 small green bell pepper, roughly chopped
1 small red bell pepper, roughly chopped
1 red or green chili, seeded, cored and cut into thin strips
½ cup chicken or vegetable broth
1 tsp sugar
1 tsp vinegar
Salt and pepper
1 tsp cornstarch
1 tbsp soy sauce
Sesame oil
6 tbsps oil

---

1. Cut the eggplant in half and score the surface.

2. Sprinkle lightly with salt and leave to drain in a colander or on paper towels for 30 minutes.

3. After 30 minutes, squeeze the eggplant gently to extract any bitter juices and rinse thoroughly

Step 1 Cut the eggplant in half and lightly score the surface.

under cold water. Pat dry and cut the eggplant into 1 inch cubes.

4. Heat about 3 tbsps oil in a wok. Add the eggplant and stir-fry about 4-5 minutes. It may be necessary to add more oil as the eggplant cooks. Remove from the wok and set aside.

5. Reheat the wok and add 2 tbsps oil. Add the garlic and ginger and stir-fry 1 minute. Add the onions and stir-fry 2 minutes. Add the bell peppers and chili pepper and stir-fry 1 minute. Return the eggplant to the wok along with the remaining ingredients.

6. Bring to the boil, stirring constantly, and cook until the sauce thickens and clears.

Index

Chili Beef Stew makes a delicious supper dish.